In Our Time

BOOKS BY ERIC HOFFER

The True Believer
The Passionate State of Mind
The Ordeal of Change
The Temper of Our Time
Working and Thinking on the Waterfront
First Things, Last Things
Reflections on the Human Condition
In Our Time

Eric Hoffer

IN OUR TIME

WILLIAM MORROW AND COMPANY, INC.

NEW YORK   1977

A Morrow Paperback Edition published by arrangement with Harper & Row, Publishers, Inc.

First Morrow Paperback Editions printing 1977.

Portions of this book have appeared in *Change* magazine.

Portions of this work originally appeared in *The New York Times.*

Printed in the United States of America.

3   4   5   6   7   8   9   10

Library of Congress Cataloging in Publication Data

Hoffer, Eric.
In our time.

    (A Cass Canfield book)
    1. Social History—20th century.   2. United
States—Social Conditions—1945–
I. Title.
HN58.H62   1976   309.1′04   76-48863

ISBN 0-688-08172-X

DESIGNED BY DOROTHY SCHMIDERER

To Steven and Eric

who have taught me much

Contents

In Our Time

What Has Not Changed in America

A disconcerting aspect of our time is that we do not know what is happening to us. Rapid, drastic change means the intrusion of the future into the present with the result that the present has become as unpredictable as the future. We do not know whether the present crisis is an ending or a beginning; whether we are descending or ascending.

Increasingly we are being separated from our past. We are a different people living in a different country, and we know that we shall become more different as time passes. There is a vague fear that even if we manage to solve all our problems we shall be less than what we have been. We shall merely survive.

Yet amidst the turmoil and dismay it is startling to discover how many vital things have not changed in America. America is still the best country for the common man. It is true that the radical-chic coteries are throwing their weight around as if they owned this country. But it is also true that common people feel most at home here. For the common man—white or black—America is the last chance and the last stop. If he can't make it here he won't make it anywhere else.

Another thing that has not changed is the ease with which we can cut ourselves off from the conformity, vulgarity, obscenity, hysterical clamor and other corrupting influences that pervade the life around us. This is still an ideal country for people who want to be left alone. And there is still plenty of elbowroom. The distant horizons are still here.

America is still an ideal country for people who want to realize their capacities and talents. Had I entered the mainstream of American life in the 1970s instead of the 1920s I would still be able to educate myself, learn to write and have books published. (It might even be easier now, since during many of my learning years I was but a step ahead of hunger.) The public libraries are still as good as they were in the past, and publishers as hospitable to a manuscript of some merit.

Certain things have improved. There is less loneliness in America. The camaraderie of the young from all walks of life and their readiness to share what they have is beautiful to behold. It is also true that enterprise and character will take a young person farther now than in the past. Alertness, willingness and reliability are quickly noticed and appreciated.

Personal relations have become more gentle and kind. There is less elbowing and pushing, and in matters that do not require moral or physical courage Americans are more ready with help.

And we have grown wiser. We now know that affluence is a threat to social stability; that the adult's failure of nerve is more critical than the young's impulse toward anarchy; that righting wrongs is a perilous undertaking which needs a tightening of social discipline; that a sense of usefulness is more vital to the quality of life than abundance or even freedom.

Dull Work

There seems to be a general assumption that brilliant people cannot stand routine; that they need a varied, exciting life in order to do their best. It is also assumed that dull people are particularly suited for dull work. We are told that the reason the present-day young protest so loudly against the dullness of factory jobs is that they are better educated and brighter than the young of the past.

Actually, there is no evidence that people who achieve much crave for, let alone live, eventful lives. The opposite is nearer the truth. One thinks of Amos the sheepherder, Socrates the stonemason, Omar the tentmaker. Jesus probably had his first revelations while doing humdrum carpentry work. Einstein worked out his theory of relativity while serving as a clerk in a Swiss patent office. Machiavelli wrote *The Prince* and the *Dis-*

courses while immersed in the dull life of a small country town where the only excitement he knew was playing cards with muleteers at the inn. Immanuel Kant's daily life was an unalterable routine. The housewives of Königsberg set their clocks when they saw him pass on his way to the university. He took the same walk each morning, rain or shine. The greatest distance Kant ever traveled was sixty miles from Königsberg.

The outstanding characteristic of man's creativeness is the ability to transmute trivial impulses into momentous consequences. The greatness of man is in what he can do with petty grievances and joys, and with common physiological pressures and hungers. "When I have a little vexation," wrote Keats, "it grows in five minutes into a theme for Sophocles." To a creative individual all experience is seminal—all events are equidistant from new ideas and insights—and his inordinate humanness shows itself in the ability to make the trivial and common reach an enormous way.

An eventful life exhausts rather than stimulates. Milton, who in 1640 was a poet of great promise, spent twenty sterile years in the eventful atmosphere of the Puritan revolution. He fulfilled his great promise when the revolution was dead, and he in solitary disgrace. Cellini's exciting life kept him from becoming the great artist he could have been. It is legitimate to doubt whether Machiavelli would have written his great books had he been allowed to continue in the diplomatic service of Florence and had he gone on interesting missions. It is usually the mediocre poets, writers, etc., who go in search of stimulating events to release their creative flow.

It may be true that work on the assembly line dulls the faculties and empties the mind, the cure only being fewer hours of work at higher pay. But during fifty years as a workingman, I have found dull routine compatible with an active mind. I can still savor the joy I used to derive from the fact that while doing dull, repetitive work on the waterfront, I could talk with my partners and compose sentences in the back of my mind, all at the same time. Life seemed glorious. Chances are that had my work been of absorbing interest I could not have done any thinking and composing on the company's time or even on my own time after returning from work.

People who find dull jobs unendurable are often dull people who do not know what to do with themselves when at leisure. Children and mature people thrive on dull routine, while the adolescent, who has lost the child's capacity for concentration and is without the inner resources of the mature, needs excitement and novelty to stave off boredom.

New Schools

Some time ago, while writing an essay on the young, I was surprised by the discovery that the young at present do not constitute a higher percentage of the population than they did in the past. The percentage of the young has remained remarkably constant through many decades. What has changed is the percentage of teen-agers.

We used to count as teen-agers those between the ages of thirteen and nineteen. Now the teen-age group includes those between the ages of ten and thirty. Television is giving ten-year-olds the style of life of juveniles, while the post-sputnik education explosion has been keeping students in their late twenties on the campuses in a state of prolonged adolescence. There are no children any more. Our public schools are packed with mini-men hungering for the prerogatives and probably the responsibilities of adults.

The poet W. H. Auden said that what America needs are puberty rites and a council of elders—which are probably beyond our reach. What this country needs and can have is child labor. The mini-men, bored by meaningless book learning, are hungry for action, hungry to acquire all kinds of skills. There will be no peace in the schools and no effective learning until the curriculum is reformed to meet the needs of the new type of students.

There is evidence that a student in his early twenties, when he is eager to learn, can master in less than a year all the book learning that teachers try to force into unwilling, bored minds through grammar and high school. There is also evidence that forced book learning in public schools, rather than preparing students for a fuller mastery of subjects later in college, often makes them unfit for it. When the great British physicist Sir Joseph Thomson was asked why England produced great scientists, he answered: "Because we hardly teach science at all in schools. Over here the minds that come to physics arrive in the laboratory with a freshness untarnished by routine." Reading and writing are a different matter—if these are not thoroughly mastered early in life we will continue to have what we have now: college students who can neither read nor write.

I propose, then, that half of the school day be given to book learning—reading and writing, elementary mathematics, a familiarization with the geography of the planet, and a bird's-eye view of history—and the other half to the mastery of skills. Retired skilled carpenters, masons, plumbers, electricians, mechanics, gardeners, architects, city planners, etc., could teach the young how to build houses and roads, how to landscape and garden, how to operate all sorts of machines. Retired bankers, manufacturers, merchants and politicians could familiarize the young with finance and management.

In small towns where there is only one school it would be easy to set aside a hundred acres or so on which generations of students could build a model neighborhood, plant gardens and raise crops. In large cities the work would have to be done on the outskirts or on land made available by slum clearance. By the time they graduated from high school the young would be equipped not only to earn a living but to run the world.

There is no reason to believe that adults will soon regain their lost nerve and be able to impose their values on the young. But there is nothing to prevent adults from transmitting their skills. It is also becoming evident that a society that does not know how to cope with juveniles can maintain the measure of stability and continuity requisite for civilized living only by abolishing adolescence—by giving the young from the age of ten the skills, opportunities, responsibilities and rewards of grownups.

A New Ruling Class

I was past middle age when the "Free Speech" movement exploded on the Berkeley Campus in 1964. Like most older people I was outraged by the sight of history made by juvenile delinquents. Yet, from the beginning, part of me was straining for a detached view. I became interested in the role the young had played in history, and it did not take much research to show me that we can hardly know how things happened in the past unless we keep in mind that much of the time it was juveniles who made them happen.

The discovery did not turn me into a champion of the young. Watching the happenings of the 1960s I shuddered at the thought of a world run by self-important, self-indulgent, self-righteous, violent and clownish punks. Nevertheless, in the 1970s I find myself now and then believing that history made by the young may help us solve some otherwise insoluble problems.

Until the middle of the nineteenth century the young were prominent in politics and acted effectively as creators of business enterprises, advocates of new philosophical doctrines and leaders of armies. The middle-aged came to the fore with the industrial revolution. The experience and capital necessary to make a successful capitalist in an industrial age required a long period of apprenticeship. One might say that from the middle of the nineteenth century the world has been run by and for the middle-aged. This era seems now to be nearing its end.

The golden century of the middle-aged was a century of colossal achievements, but also of unprecedented global exploitation and global wars. In no other era have the young been sacrificed so recklessly by their elders. And the middle-aged were bunglers as history makers. Does anyone believe that the course of history would have been any more destructive had the young of the warring nations come together in 1919 and written a peace treaty instead of leaving peacemaking to the middle-aged and the old?

The most fateful fact at this moment is that over half the population of the planet is under twenty-five—an age group that clamors for action and power. In the past, the predominance of the young coincided with a short life span: the young had opportunities for action because the older people were eliminated by death.

Today, longevity combined with the driving creativity of the young produce an explosive situation. But we need not adopt Stalin's practice of killing the old to make room for the young. Instead, we could have an upper age limit for holding public office. We could retire people at forty.

In an age of ceaseless change people over forty are no longer flexible enough to take things in their stride. Feeling the strain, they may not mind stepping back. They can stand the separation from action and power much better than the young, bursting with energy and driven by the need to prove themselves. And, should compulsory retirement breed frustration and bitterness, it stands to reason that people over forty would have neither the energy nor the recklessness to tear the world apart.

Retirement at forty would have to be linked with an earlier start for adulthood—say at thirteen. But after doing the everyday world's work for twenty-seven years one would gain entrance into another world of creative leisure. For it is likely that retirement at forty would result in something like a cultural renaissance. People over forty are more attuned to learning and more patient in application than the young. The need to compensate themselves in the realm of thought and imagination for what they have had to give up in the world of action ought to generate a potent creative ferment. One would also expect a flowering of scholarship when the over-forty go back to the universities to mesh what they have learned in the book of the world with what they can find in the world of books.

Finally, the camaraderie now present among young people of all walks of life, all nations and all races gives the hope of peace and amity between classes, nations and races in a world ruled by the young.

A Meaningful Life

One of the lessons of the 1960s has been that abundance, freedom, equality and justice are not the most vital ingredients of a satisfactory individual existence. We begin to realize that from now on a society will be able to stay on an even keel only when it makes it possible for a majority of its people to live meaningful lives.

Now, there is no doubt that in a modern society there is not enough meaningful work to make it possible for most people to derive the meaning in their lives from the work they do to earn a living. For it is a peculiarity of a modern society that the existence of millions depends on being paid for doing what seems like nothing when done. The demand that the work we do for a living should be worth doing, though not "a human impertinence," as Santayana thinks, is unrealizable.

There is a widely held assumption that the way to inject meaning into an individual existence is by participation in communal affairs. Good citizenship, it is true, involves a concern for the welfare of one's community, one's country and probably of humanity in general. But to make such a concern the main content of an individual life is, in normal times, unnatural and unhealthy. With the majority of people, participation in communal affairs cannot be more than a condiment.

In a healthy society the craving for acting with others becomes an aid to the realization and cultivation of the individual. One joins others in a relatively small circle to learn a skill, master a subject or exercise a talent. It is the acquisition of skills in particular, irrespective of their utility, that is potent in making life meaningful. Since man has no inborn skills, the survival of the species has depended on the ability to acquire and perfect skills. Hence the mastery of skills is a uniquely human activity and yields deep satisfaction.

I am also convinced that the mastery of skills can be therapeutic. Skill-healing should be particularly effective in the reconstruction and human renewal of the chronically poor, the unemployable and people who cannot cope with life. The acquisition of a skill generates confidence and, since people enjoy doing what they are good at, it may have an energizing effect.

Were I the mayor of San Francisco, I would have a square or a street lined with small shops where subsidized experts would practice and display every imaginable skill. I would comb the globe for little-known or half-forgotten skills in order to revive them. And I would have children apprenticed to the experts. It is most fitting that in an automated world the human hand, a most unique organ, should come back into its own and again perform wonders. It may well be the hand that will save us.

A Job to Do

You ask yourself: What are the essential attributes a country must have if it is to remain vigorous? The answer is simple: So long as a country has courage and a passion for excellence it can face the future confidently no matter how fearsome its difficulties. Courage is not only a serviceable substitute for hope but also, as we shall see, a chief factor in the maintenance of personal security. As to the passion for excellence, it may sound highfalutin, but it actually concerns common, everyday affairs. I have spent fifty years doing backbreaking work in the fields, in lumber camps and on the waterfront. Many of the people I lived and worked with had courage and, whether they knew it or not, a passion for excellence.

The word "job" used to have a magical connotation in this country. It was something you had to do the best way you knew how. A job might be unpleasant, dangerous or trivial, but it still had to be done, and it had a claim on your skill and ingenuity. Even the simplest job had its mysteries; and once you fathomed them, time flew.

As one would expect, the formula "There is a job to do" cropped up in situations that had nothing to do with work. The American's performance on the battlefield, for instance, had a matter-of-fact, job-doing quality. He did not fight for a motherland, a fatherland or some ideal. There was a job to do and he did it. Field Marshal Rommel was astonished by the prosaic, practical manner in which Americans mastered modern warfare.

The manner in which the word "job" lost its magical potency illustrates the irony of history. I remember how scornful I felt when I first read Marx's description of the worker's attitude toward work in a capitalist society. The worker, he said, feels physically and morally debased by his work. He is like an exile in his place of work and feels at home only when away from his job. Marx never did a day's work in his life, and never took the trouble to find out how a worker really feels when on the job. He naturally assumed that workers were a lesser breed of intellectuals. Yet one hundred years after Marx, by an ironic twist of history, a toylike sputnik launched in Marxist Russia set off a chain of events which eventually made Marx's false diagnosis come true in capitalist America.

On October 4, 1957, the Russians placed a medicine-ball-sized satellite in orbit, and we woke up to discover that the clodhopping, backward Russians were ahead of us. We reacted hysterically. Catching up was a new and frightening experience. We poured billions of dollars into universities to produce scientists and technicians wholesale. There were soon seven million university students, and this mass of semester intellectuals set the tone for the young in every walk of life.

By now American workers have indeed become a lesser breed of intellectuals, and their attitude toward work fits Marx's description. They feel demeaned and dehumanized by the work they have to do, and see a job as a trap. Workingmen who have never read a book talk glibly about frustration, alienation and relevance. Like intellectuals, they expect a job not only to give them the wherewithal of a living but to fill their lives with meaning.

The fact that the word "job" has lost its magic is affecting America's performance and style in every field. Will we now need the tribal magic of charismatic leaders and medicine men to get things done in peacetime and in war?

Morale

Low morale is our central problem at present. Low morale in factories and offices, in homes and schools, in government and in the armed forces. Most educated people I talk with tell me that what we need is a great leader. I tell them that ours is not a time of leaders. Right now there is not one outstanding leader anywhere on this planet. The situation is paradoxical. The twentieth century has been a century of leaders, much more so than the nineteenth. Yet it is beginning to look as though the last quarter of this century will not be favorable for the emergence of great leaders.

What has happened? The two world wars produced only one great leader—Churchill. Almost all the other great leaders of this century appeared in the aftermath of the wars, and their emergence was linked with the building or rebuilding of nations. It would seem by application of this rule there are at the moment only two countries—Britain and Italy—with a situation ripe for the coming of a great leader. Although the potential exists in parts of Asia, Africa, and Latin America, there is a tendency at present for a military junta to take over when social chaos erupts. On the other hand, in the Western democracies as long as a country goes on functioning tolerably well it cannot expect an exceptional leader to solve its pressing problems or give it hope and faith.

Nor can we look to ideology as a generator of morale. In the modern Occidental world, where individuality has deep roots, dedication to leaders or holy causes cannot have a durable hold on people. In Japan, emperor worship produced soldiers who fought to the last breath and never surrendered. Something similar may take place in China. But in the Occident faith is perishable. The superb performance of the German soldier in the Second World War was not due mainly to Nazi indoctrination. Here is a passage from the diary of a German officer cadet who died on the Russian front in September 1943: "Why does one stand all this? Is it for the Führer, the Fatherland and one's people? No, no, a thousand times no! It is only because one's comrades are in the same boat and one must not forsake them. That is the reason, nothing else!"

Esprit de corps is what remains when faith and dedication evaporate. Particularly in the present intellectual climate, the spirit that binds a relatively small number of people into something like a family is perhaps the only durable source of morale. How to implant and cultivate this "esprit" is the vital task facing all countries in the Occident. Even so, it is my impression that little has been written on the subject. The people who know how to create esprit de corps, whether in the army or in places of work, are usually not good with words.

The other day I had a glimpse of esprit de corps in action. I happened to be in the first-class compartment of a United Airlines plane flying nonstop from Chicago to San Francisco. Recently I have noticed that on long flights the first-class compartment has only 10 to 20 percent of its seats occupied. But this time every seat was taken. An old couple, the man walking with difficulty, were ushered to their seats with extra care by the stewardesses and one of the pilots. I noticed that many of the passengers knew each other. Across the aisle from me an elderly man was dictating something to a youngish man, who covered page after page of a large writing pad. Little by little it dawned on me that most of the first-class passengers were United Airline employees—present and past. The old man who received the royal treatment was a retired pilot—one of the earliest and perhaps something of a legend. I had a chance to ask the oldish man across the aisle whether he was dictating a speech. He told me he used to work for

United but was now raising apples in Vermont. The youngish fellow next to him was a lawyer working for the airline. He was involved in a difficult case and was picking the brain of the older man, who knew something about it. Clearly, United Airlines knows how to create family ties among its employees. In a family sons can ask fathers for advice and there are grandparents to cherish. Once you see esprit de corps as family-forming you can think of many obvious and subtle ways to advance it.

Though ours is not a time of great leaders, it yet offers abundant opportunities for persons who have something extra—a touch of grace, a sparkle, the competence to see a job through. These persons are very much like everyone else and do not occupy a position of leadership, but their presence is crucial in the creation of esprit de corps.

A Substitute for Illusion

You can count on the fingers of one hand the countries
that are at present threatened by war. The contrast
with the situation that prevailed as recently as the early
1960s is striking. Nationalism, which we feared as an
explosive that would blow us to high heaven, is now at
an all-time low in the Occident, where it originated.

I cannot think of anyone who foresaw this startling
development. But even more surprising have been the
consequences of this relaxation of international tensions. The world has not become more peaceful and
secure. Indeed, never before have so many countries
been in deep trouble. Instead of the traditional threat
of war, societies are now faced with the unfamiliar
threat of internal disruption. The fate of a nation is now
decided not on the battlefield but in the streets of big
cities, in factories, mines and fields, and on the cam-

puses of universities. Moreover, internal strife is gathering force at a time when most people are better off than they have been in the past.

Obviously, war, nationalism and scarcity are sources of social cohesion and discipline. We tend to forget that social bodies were to begin with organs of struggle: struggle with external enemies, and struggle to wrest a livelihood from grudging nature. Hence in a time like ours, when the possibility of abundance goes hand in hand with an absence of external threats, social cohesion is bound to diminish. There is total demobilization and a discarding of discipline. It is a paradox of the human condition that the longed for end of war and of want should bring societies to the brink of anarchy.

We are living in an epoch of great disillusionment. We are beginning to suspect that to fulfill a hope is to defeat it, and to make a dream come true is to turn it into a nightmare. For a moment it seemed to us that we had arrived, that we had solved all material problems and could sit back and enjoy an eternal sabbath. But we are discovering that the more triumphant our technology, the less does society function automatically. In a time of widespread automation nothing happens automatically. You have to push and pull, threaten and beg if you want anything done. It seems that by mastering matter we have drained material factors of their potency to shape events. Look what has happened to money! Money cannot induce people to work harder or

longer hours. Money cannot cure chronic poverty.
Money cannot buy personal security. It was a shock to
a materialistic civilization to discover that the most im-
portant facts about a human entity are its illusions, its
fictions, its unfounded convictions. A society without
illusions is without vigor and without order and continuity. It took a triumphant technology to demonstrate
that "things which are not are mightier than things that
are."

In the past illusions were not only long-lived, but the
fading of one illusion automatically heightened the
receptivity to a new one. But right now in the Western
world illusions no longer have the power to lure people
to strenuous effort. Life is no longer as visibly miserable
as it was in the past, and the opportunities for full-
bodied fun easily outbid the appeal of a distant hope.
The question is how a population wholly oriented
toward the present can be induced to submit to the
self-denial indispensable for social cohesion and discipline. Is there a substitute for illusion?

It is probably true that at present workingmen are
the most disillusioned segment of the population. No
matter how high the wages and how generous the
fringe benefits, the feeling persists that all a workingman can get out of his job is a living, and he is in it for
life. The prospect before him is an endless daily grind,
an endless deadening routine which so bruises body and
mind that retirement at sixty-five means a mere fading
out.

The spreading revulsion from work can be counteracted only by offering the workingman a tangible and relatively immediate goal. Assuming that a year has 240 working days of six hours each, then twenty years of work—4,800 days—should qualify a worker for a pension. A day in the mine or on the assembly line should count double and so should overtime work. Under such an arrangement, a youth who started working at eighteen would have (counting overtime) a fair chance of retiring at thirty-five or so. If he became a miner or worked on the assembly line he could retire sooner. Moreover, a six-hour workday might make it possible for many to get an education while they were working. Two hours of book learning a day should give a workingman a college education by the time he retires.

A Learning Society

No one will maintain that exceptional people are needed to make a great nation. The Russians lick the boots of their oppressors, betray close friends and even relatives, and cannot tell falsehood from truth. They move and yell and salivate to order. Yet Russia is a great nation with outstanding achievements in many fields. Or take Germany. The German historian Theodor Mommsen said of Bismarck that he made Germany great and the Germans small. Here, again, we have a great nation and small people.

It is true that both Russia and Germany achieved greatness without freedom. Is the situation different in nations with a tradition of freedom? Hardly so. It was largely the outcasts and undesirables from Europe who tamed our savage continent and helped make America great. So, too, the immigrants and soldiers who built the British Empire were recruited from the dregs of England.

Early in the nineteenth century the poet Coleridge urged his fellow Englishmen: "Let us become a better people and all else shall be added unto us." Perhaps the only legitimate purpose of achieving national greatness is to make it possible for a great nation to become a better people.

How do we become a better people, and what is the "all else" that shall be added unto us?

To me a good society is a society in which most people have the desire and the opportunities to learn and grow. It is a society in which schools produce not learned but learning people. It is a society in which people have neither the time nor the inclination to exploit or oppress or otherwise harm their fellow men. Moreover, it is reasonable to expect that in a learning society not only will there not be a gap between generations, but people of different capacities and bents will come together, commune with, emulate and encourage each other, and thus create an optimal milieu for the realization of talents. I shall, therefore, rephrase Coleridge and say: Let us become a learning people and all else shall be added unto us. The "all else" is the full unfolding of our creative endowments.

It is indeed remarkable how many of our present difficulties would be mitigated or even removed in a learning society. It is plausible, for instance, that a learning society would have a decided advantage in a time of rapid change: while the learned usually find themselves equipped to live in a world that no longer exists, the learner adjusts himself readily to all sorts of conditions. It is also plausible that a learning society would be immune to the perils of affluence. Up to now in free societies social discipline has been a by-product of scarcity, and the turbulent 1960s have shown us that the most urgent need of an affluent society is a new source of discipline. Learning could be such a source since the learner is a disciplined person. Finally, a learning society would be an ideal milieu for the old. To learn is to grow, and those who grow do not grow old.

As a nation made up largely of the descendants of immigrants, we probably have a special aptitude for learning. The immigrants had to learn a new language and a new way of life. They had to keep on learning in order to survive. It was this readiness to learn which made possible the integration of heterogenous immigrants into one nation.

A Return to the Past?

Although it seems reasonable to expect a post-Christian world to revert in some degree to pre-Christian paganism, hardly anyone is hospitable to the idea that post-industrial society might revert in some degree to pre-industrial days. What kinship could there be between an automated affluent society and a hand-run society immersed in scarcity? Yet even a cursory reading of the social history of the early decades of the nineteenth century reveals startling similarities with our time. The London and Paris of those days had the same insoluble problems that at present confront our big cities. There were slums, overcrowding and violent crime in the streets. The well-to-do middle class became obsessed with the new dangers and the explosive social situation. The nightly muggings, beatings and holdups were the chief topic of conversation. The poor were seen not simply as people without money but as a race of savages and barbarians. There was also a chorus of complaints from employers about the indolence and negligence of workers. There was a stubborn resistance among workers to dull, repetitive factory work. Coleridge observed in 1833 that in Manchester and Birmingham "the most skillful artisans are constantly in the habit of working but a few days a week and idling the rest." Absenteeism was high, especially on Mondays, and the high turnover of labor crippled production. It all echoes what is happening right now in the automobile factories of Detroit, U.S.A., and of Coventry, England.

In nineteenth-century England the reconciliation of the working population with factory routine occurred in the late 1840s, in the wake of the railroad boom. Railroad-building stimulated a whole range of new metal industries which, unlike the textile mills, employed only men and paid high wages. Around 1850 the illusion was born that there was a comfortable, secure middle-class existence ahead for the steady worker. The illusion lasted until the Great Depression of the 1930s, when the conviction spread among unemployed workers on the dole that hard, steady work does not get one anywhere.

It is remarkable that whereas books on the coming of the industrial revolution usually have a clear recognition that the willingness to work, as much as anything else, gave modern civilization its unique character and marked it off from all its predecessors, there is rarely a reference to the changed attitude toward work in books on post-industrial society. They mention the educational attainments of the new generation of workers, the shift from blue-collar to white-collar work, the role of the unions, but not a word about an impending human-energy crisis. So axiomatic is the assumption that history is made by elites that it simply does not enter the forecaster's mind that a revulsion from work is likely to give the post-industrial society a backward pre-industrial aspect.

It seems specially fitting that the end of the drama of industrialization and modernization should be enacted most strikingly in the country where it began. In Britain the denouement is unfolding with the inevitability of fate. Nowhere else is it so clearly evident that the present crisis is not due mainly to the quadrupling of the price of oil. If by 1980 oil from the bottom of the North Sea should make Britain rich, it would only become an Anglo-Saxon Saudi Arabia.

The Middle Class

We cannot know how things really happened in history unless we know who it was that made them happen. The most crucial fact about the machine age is that it has been the creation of the middle class. It is indeed doubtful whether any other human type could have originated a machine age. One of the reasons that Chinese civilization, with all its ingenuity and inventiveness, did not evolve an industrial system is that it did not favor the emergence of a full-blown middle class. Confucianism valued the peasant and the country above the trader and the town, and hindered the growth of a Chinese bourgeoisie. It is also significant that when in the last third of the nineteenth century the British middle classes embraced the values and the style of life of the aristocracy, the machine age in Britain began to lose its dynamism. The drive that should have gone into ceaseless industrial innovation and expansion was diverted by middle-class statesmen into the aristocratic pastime of empire building. In Germany and Japan the machine age gained its full swing only after the Second World War, when the middle classes at last came into their own. On the other hand, a Russia dominated by doctrinaire commissars has remained industrially backward despite its sputniks. A middle class is needed not only to originate a machine age but to operate it effectively.

Early in the nineteenth century, Count Claude Henri de Saint-Simon characterized the coming of the industrial revolution as a passage from the management of men to the administration of things. Now, the middle class is the only human type more interested in, and better equipped for, the mastery of things than the management of men. Aristocrats, intellectuals, priests, soldiers and even common people prize influence over men more highly than the power to move mountains and tell rivers whither to flow. The middle class manages men awkwardly and is happiest when the hidden hand of circumstance does the managing. It has to utilize the magic of the intellectual in the manipulation of customers, and the aristocratic tradition in the management of soldiers. As a ruling class, the middle class stands alone in its refusal to employ sheer force or magic to cope with the complexity of human nature. It by-passes human nature by hugging the assumption that people will operate tolerably well when left to themselves.

The events of the 1960s have shown that when the middle class is no longer immersed in a struggle with nature, when it has solved the problems of production, and abundance is within reach, it becomes unsure of its footing and seems to have nowhere to go. Its values, based on scarcity, begin to disintegrate and it no longer feels itself in possession of the true and only view possible for sensible people. The middle class is unprepared and unequipped to lead people to Eden, and it cannot find a substitute for the social automatism induced by unfulfilled needs and fear of want. Finally, because of its trivial motivation, the middle class cannot win and hold the young who absorb the clichés and slogans of alienated intellectuals, with their clamor for meaningful, weighty lives.

Thus we are witnessing the decline and fall of the middle class. Would-be charismatic leaders are preening themselves in the wings, and medicine men are rehearsing incantations. But the end of the trivial, mean-souled middle class that would sell its soul for cash will probably mean the end of civility, of tolerance, and perhaps of laughter.

Money

Most of us spend much of our time satisfying other people's needs. To a visitor from another planet it would seem that human beings, like bees, are engaged in selfless toil. It would take him some time to discover that this self-sacrificing behavior is induced by a magic drug called money.

Whoever originated the cliché that money is the root of all evil knew hardly anything about the nature of evil and very little about human beings. The monstrous evils of the twentieth century have shown us that the greediest money grubbers are gentle doves compared with money-hating wolves like Lenin, Stalin and Hitler, who in less than three decades killed or maimed nearly a hundred million men, women and children, and brought untold suffering to a large portion of mankind.

The middle class was relatively harmless as a ruling

class because money could cure all that ailed it. But the passage from the nineteenth to the twentieth century saw a shift from a preoccupation with money to a preoccupation with power, and centuries ago Sir Francis Bacon saw such a shift as "the origin of all evil."

It is part of the sickness of our time that money has lost its magic power. What ails societies at present is not that everybody wants as much money as possible but that everybody wants to do as little as possible. We used to wonder how in the nineteenth century it was possible for so few to have so much at the expense of the many. Now the wonder is that so many get so much at the expense of the few. A showdown between the few who work and the many who don't will make a strange sort of revolution.

What will life be like in a society without money? Men will try to assert and prove themselves by all sorts of means and under all sorts of conditions. The question is what means for the demonstration of individual worth are likely to develop in a nonacquisitive society. Vying in creativeness is not a likely substitute for vying in acquisitiveness—not only because creativity is accessible to the relatively few, but because creative work is without automatic recognition and is not easily measured. Rather, the nonacquisitive society is likely to develop into a combination of army and school. People will prove themselves by winning degrees, medals and rank. There will be as much, if not more, self-seeking, envy and malice as in a moneyed society.

A society without money will be largely preoccupied with managing people. There will be little social automatism. Sowing, harvesting, mining, manufacturing, etc., will become burning national problems. Instead of the harmless drug of money there will be the black magic of brainwashing and soul-raping. Eventually the medicine men will be replaced by slave drivers.

What Capitalism Cannot Do

We know by now what capitalism and communism can and cannot do.

Capitalism can produce abundance. It gives full scope to the energies of the individual, and is an optimal milieu for people who can help themselves and want to be left alone. But capitalism cannot do much for the helpless. It cannot turn the chronically poor into active, useful citizens. Nor does it know how to cope with people who are more interested in quality of life than in a high standard of living.

Communism cannot create abundance, and it cannot release a copious flow of spontaneous energies. It cannot utilize the energies of enterprising people who are at their best when left to themselves. But communism can do wonders with the chronically poor. It also appeals to people who crave to live weighty, momentous lives.

Capitalism's disconcerting predicament is that it gets in trouble when it achieves abundance. Capitalist society is strained to the breaking point not, as Marx predicted, by ever-increasing misery, but by affluence. Once scarcity has been eliminated, capitalism does not know how to induce people to work. Moreover, the erosion of the pre-capitalist authorities of family, church and school leaves capitalism helpless in the face of social anarchy. By itself, capitalism cannot foster a communal spirit; it cannot generate the social discipline and cohesion requisite for civilized living.

The indications are that neither capitalism nor communism can endure as a pure system. The beauty of it is that a capitalist society incorporating communist elements can have smoother sailing than a communist society incorporating capitalist elements. The capitalist elements in a communist society are likely to be more corrosive and subversive than the communist elements in a capitalist society.

What, then, are the collectivist approaches a capitalist society might employ in order to do things it cannot do on its own? First, the chronically poor. David Pender of the University of South Carolina has advocated the resettling of the chronically poor in cooperative hamlets on the periphery of the big cities where skilled advisers would teach them how to produce vegetables, fruit, eggs and milk. They would go on receiving undiminished welfare checks, and whatever they get from the cooperative marketing of their produce would be an added bonus. Eventually these hamlets might produce enough to feed the cities, and in the process the chronically poor might be changed from psychological cripples into self-respecting individuals capable of holding their own in any society. There would be sweet irony in using communism to prepare people for capitalism.

Similarly, the present hostility to work on the assembly line might be overcome by having large communes of workers associated with privately owned factories. These large kibbutzim would not only satisfy the young's present hunger for a communal way of life, but by requiring their members to raise their own food, build their own buildings, make their own furniture and run their own schools, they would give them all sorts of opportunities for meaningful work. In addition, each member would be obliged to work two or three days a week on the assembly line in the adjoining factory.

Private Enterprise
Russian Style

It is curious that the finest examples of communal living are found in the kibbutzim of noncommunist Israel, while nowhere are the virtues of private enterprise so clearly demonstrated as on the private plots of land worked by collectivized peasants in Communist Russia. These private plots, about two-thirds of an acre in size, add up to less than 3 percent of Russia's arable land, and the peasants work on them only in their spare time, yet they produce about half of Russia's meat, milk and green vegetables and about four-fifths of its eggs and potatoes. It is significant that the men and women who perform this miracle of production are the descendants of the lesser peasants who were left on the land after the more enterprising peasants had been liquidated or exiled during collectivization.

The productivity of the collective farms worked by

the same peasants is strikingly low. According to Khrushchev, the output per collective worker in grain was about one-seventh that of the United States, in potatoes one-fifth, in milk one-third, in beef one-fourteenth, and so on. One of the reasons offered for this low productivity is "the siphoning off of the young, the energetic, the ambitious into city industries and professions." Yet on their private plots these inferior, left-behind peasants are performing miracles. It is obvious that in the case of Russian peasants private enterprise is an unequaled energizer. It more effectively evokes their love, imagination and care than do the lofty ideals and noble goals proclaimed by their statesmen. It is conceivable that resentment against the collective bureaucratic monstrosity also plays a part—the private plots are a refuge.

The collective farms of Israel are as productive as farms in technologically advanced small countries such as Belgium, Holland and Denmark. Moreover, their output per worker is 34 percent higher than on privately owned Israeli farms. With 3.7 percent of the Jewish population, the kibbutzim are producing half of Israel's food.

Unlike the lesser peasants who work wonders on their tiny plots in Russia, the members of the kibbutzim are in many senses a superior breed. The kibbutzim were started by well-educated, idealistic Jews who wanted to escape the banality, dishonesty and ruthlessness of the marketplace. They wanted to create a new Jew—earth-bound, hard-working and selfless. They also hoped that the ideal society they were building would serve as a model for the rest of mankind. It is not surprising that the kibbutzim have given Israel many of its leaders in politics, the economy and the armed forces. One has the feeling that the kibbutz can serve as a model for people who are above the average. For the common run of humanity, private enterprise is not only a natural and unexceptional mode of life, but it is also optimal for the release of their energies.

I can see how in the not too distant future a Russia turned benevolent might send delegations to Israel in order to learn how to build a communistic society that is free and democratic. On the other hand, an America that has been spending billions on unsuccessful poverty programs would do well to send delegations to Soviet Russia to learn from the lesser peasants how to turn millions of chronically poor Americans into enterprising human beings. We could even invite hundreds of these peasants to come over and teach our poor by example.

Fifty-some years after the Russian Revolution, it is still questionable whether the Russians have an aptitude for communistic living. No one inside or outside Russia believes that left to themselves the Russian people would maintain unaltered the present communist system. On the other hand, the performance of the

Russian peasants on their private plots, and the ingenuity and fortitude displayed by Russian black marketeers, suggest that the Russian people have a passion and an aptitude for private enterprise. Russian capitalism before the First World War showed an exceptional vigor. The tempo of industrialization between 1887 and 1912 was such that competent observers expected Russia to catch up and perhaps overtake Western European countries by the middle of the century.

One wonders whether the men in the Kremlin might not be forced to make use of this Russian predilection for private enterprise to secure Eastern Siberia against China. The fate of Eastern Siberia will be decided by Russia's ability to pack it with thirty million hustling immigrants. This could be achieved most easily and rapidly by turning Eastern Siberia into an America of the late nineteenth century—free, and with fabulous opportunities for individual self-advancement. Come and get it!

The Trader

It seems strange that we know so little of the history of
the trader. The trader preceded the cultivator and the
herder, and he is probably more ancient than the
hunter and the warrior.

The trader and the artist are probably of equal antiquity, and the most uniquely human. There are animal hunters and warriors, and some ant species engage
in activities reminiscent of cultivating and herding, but
nowhere in the animal world is there anything
remotely equivalent to the trader and the artist.

That early man, so naked to the elements and preda-
tors, should have survived at all seems miraculous. But
the situation becomes doubly miraculous when we find
that earliest man was the only lighthearted being in a
deadly serious universe, given to playing and tinkering,
and exerting himself more in the pursuit of superfluities

than of necessities. He had ornaments before he had clothing, and clay figurines before clay pots. From his earliest beginning man was a luxury-loving animal, and the earliest trade was in luxuries. Trade in necessities was a late development.

The trader was probably the first individual. He became an individual not by choice but by circumstances. He was either a straggler left behind or a fugitive or a sole survivor. Earliest trade was foreign trade, and the trader was a foreigner. Even at present in backward parts of the world most traders are foreigners: Indians in East Africa, Lebanese and Greeks in West Africa, Parsees in India, and Chinese in Southeast Asia. I can see the first trader, an outsider, approaching a strange human group, bearing a gift of something new and desirable, and then going on from group to group exchanging gifts.

Considering the trader's antiquity and the vital role he played in the evolution of civilization, it is difficult to understand the scorn and disdain he evoked in other human types, particularly in the warrior and the scribe. To the warrior who made history and the scribe who recorded it, the trader was the embodiment of greed, dishonesty, cowardice, dishonor, mendacity and corruption in general. Yet it was the trader who first gave weapons to the warrior and the craft of writing to the scribe. Traders' tags and marks of ownership preceded clay tablets and papyrus rolls. Later, when the scribe had made writing so cumbersome and complex that one needed a lifetime to master it, the Phoenician trader moved in to simplify it by introducing the phonetic alphabet.

The age-old enmity between warrior and trader becomes particularly intriguing when seen in the light of recent events which indicate a kinship between the two so close as to make possible an interchange of roles. We have seen German and Japanese warriors become the world's foremost traders, and the Jews foremost warriors.

As to the antagonism between the trader and the scribe: Where the trader is in power, the scribe is usually kept out of the management of affairs, but is given a free hand in the cultural field. By frustrating the scribe's craving for commanding action the trader draws upon himself the scribe's scorn, but he also releases the scribe's creative powers. It was not a mere accident that the Hebrew prophets, the Ionian philosophers, Zoroaster, Confucius and Buddha made their appearance at a time when the trader was in ascendance. The same is of course true of the beginning of the Renaissance, and of the cultural flowering in modern times.

Where the scribe is in power, the trader is regulated and regimented off the face of the earth. In scribe-dominated communist countries the legitimate trader has been liquidated, leaving only the clandestine traders, the true revolutionaries, who undermine and frustrate totalitarian domination.

In free societies, the tug of war between trader and scribe has had beneficent effects. The trader cracked the scribe's monopoly of learning by diffusing literacy through popular education, while the scribe has been in the forefront of every movement that set out to separate the trader from his wealth. As a result, both learning and riches have leaked out to wider sections of the population.

The Trend Toward Anarchy

The present trend toward anarchy has its source in the activities of minorities. Minuscule minorities are responsible for the lack of safety in the streets, and for anarchic manifestations in schools, factories, the marketplace, and also in politics, literature and the arts.

About a hundred years ago, the historian Jakob Burckhardt had a premonition of impending chaos caused by the intrusion of the masses onto the stage of history. The masses, he thought, loathed stability and continuity; they wanted something to happen all the time, and their clamor for change would topple everything that was noble and precious. There were others, well into the twentieth century, who, like Burckhardt, saw the masses as the womb of anarchy. To Freud it seemed that "the individuals composing the masses support one another in giving free rein to their indiscipline." Not one of these learned people had an inkling that the coming anarchy would originate in tiny minorities, including a minority of the learned. Everything that has been said in the past about the anarchic propensity of the masses fits perfectly the activities of students, professors, writers, artists and their hangers-on during the 1960s, whereas the masses are now the protagonists of stability, of continuity and of law and order.

Ours is a golden age of minorities. At no time in the past have dissident minorities felt so much at home and had so much room to throw their weight around. They speak and act as if they were "the people," and what they abominate most is the dissent of the majority. The self-assertion of the majority, except on election day, is seen as a threat to freedom. It used to be that minorities looked over their shoulders wondering what the majority thought of them. Now it is the majority that wonders what the minorities think. Social scientists have been promoting the idea that disruptive minorities are but the symptom of a malady that has its root causes in the selfishness and intolerance of the majority.

The trouble is that the intimidation of the majority is occurring at a time when traditional authority has lost its effectiveness. The great revelation of the 1960s was that the power structure is manned by toothless lions. And since the failure of nerve of those in command is such that a revitalization of traditional authority remains problematical, some counterbalance must be found to the disruptive minorities if we are going to have the minimum of personal safety and social discipline requisite for civilized living. It seems to me that the choice is between an activated, vigorous majority and a replacement of traditional authority by despotic power.

An Association of Victims

Almost without exception, social scientists are telling us that Americans are now more violent than in the past. They cite statistics. Yet anyone who observes the goings on in the cities with his own eyes knows that it is not so. The American man in the street is now infinitely less pugnacious, less ready to take offense and hit back, than in the past. We used to fight in the streets, in saloons and on the job. You had to watch what you said lest you have your teeth knocked in. But just now the majority of Americans are afraid to open their mouths. They will not get into a fight no matter what you call them or do to them. They are afraid to get angry.

I maintain that it is this unprecedented meekness of the majority that is responsible for the phenomenal increase of violence. Social order is the by-product of an equilibrium between a vigorous majority and violent minorities. There is no reason to believe that the nature of the violent minorities is now greatly different from what it was in the past. What has changed is the will and the ability of the majority to react. I do not think it possible to reform the violent minorities by passing more laws, hiring more policemen or reforming the courts. We can make headway only by activating the majority.

The question is how to rouse the majority without resorting to vigilantism. I would start with the old. Violent crimes in the streets are committed largely by young punks, and nine times out of ten the victims are old men and women. The young thugs stalk the old like animals stalking their prey. They not only rob but brutally beat their victims. Now, there are all sorts of organizations that concern themselves with safeguarding the constitutional rights of the criminal, but the victims are ignored and forgotten. The victim has no civil rights, no constitutional guarantees, no Civil Liberties Union to plead his case, no one to succor him in distress and no newspapers to chronicle his agony. A recent poll showed that one in three urban residents has been mugged or robbed. And considering that the fear of violence can be as debilitating as violence, one might say that we are now a nation of victims. Anyone, therefore, who launches an organization of victims will make a good start in activating the majority.

An association of victims would have a large member-

ship of blacks. This is of crucial importance. Seventy-
five percent of the mugging and molesting in big cities
is done by Negro punks. It has been getting so that in
the public mind the words "mugger" and "Negro" have
become synonymous. Yet over half the victims of violent crime are also black. There is no doubt that any
attempt to stop violent crime must be directed mainly
against Negro juveniles; hence only an organization
with a large Negro membership could make this attempt without being suspected of racism.

I said that you start to activate the majority by organizing the old. The old are not only the typical victims
of our society, but they are also least likely to resort to
vigilante action. There could be a network of lookout
stations manned by old people equipped with binocu-
lars and walkie-talkies. They would report to a police
robbery center any suspicious goings on in the back-
yards.

One of the tasks of an association of victims would be
to make courage fashionable by honoring and celebrat-
ing those who defy malefactors. Several times a year
mayors of cities should award medals of courage. We
need shopkeepers and bank tellers who will defy
holdup men. We need citizens who will fly at a mugger's throat. We need women who will scratch and bite
and gouge out the eyes of anyone who molests them.
We need people who will explode in anger at foul-
mouthed insults and threats.

In the past, the rousing of the majority was characteristic of a time of upheaval. But in the present world,
where traditional authority is losing its effectiveness, an
activated majority is vital to the orderly flow of everyday life. I am also convinced that without a vigorous
majority we shall not be able to solve the pressing problem of racial integration. The Left has been operating
on the assumption that to speed up racial integration
you must soften up the white majority and beat it into
a pulp. But the Left has always been ignorant of the
working of man's soul. A beaten and frightened white
majority shrinks back and takes flight; it is not hospitable to outsiders lest it have its identity blurred. It was
a majority confident of its values and with unbounded
faith in its destiny that absorbed and assimilated thirty
million immigrants in the few decades before the First
World War.

The Invisible Power

Through most of history writers and artists were at their best and felt wholly at home in aristocratic societies. Achievement in the realm of thought and imagination is apparently nourished by a sense of grandeur, by seeing life as a soul-stirring drama or spectacle. "The human heart," wrote D. H. Lawrence, "needs, needs, needs splendor, gorgeousness, pride, assumption, glory and lordship. Perhaps it needs these more than it needs love; at least even more than bread." Often in the past cultural creativeness was in full vigor where poets, writers, artists and scientists were courted by the mighty.

The eighteenth century was the golden age of the alliance between men of letters and aristocrats. In the salons of that era writers and thinkers of every sort mingled on equal terms with members of the aristocracy. The intellectuals acquired the polish and urbanity of men of the world while the aristocrats, old and young, acquired a taste for the play of ideas. Conversation became the most absorbing pastime, and the ideas expressed in the salons had unexpected effects. Necker said of the salons that they formed "the invisible power which without finances and without troops imposed its law upon the town, the court, and even the king himself."

In the nineteenth century everything changed. Writers, artists and their hangers-on became exiles in their own country and were at odds with the established order. For the first time in history writers and artists ceased to have the same values as the ruling class.

The French Revolution had sent a wave of elation through the "Republic of Letters." It had seemed that intellect was to become the director and arbiter of human destinies, and men of intellect were to be in the saddle. Though some of the intellectuals were eventually disillusioned by the revolution and its Napoleonic aftermath, no one doubted that men of intellect would dominate the new century; that they would constitute the new aristocracy. Heine declared blatantly: "Mark this ye proud men of action; ye are nothing but unconscious instruments of men of thought who, often in the humblest seclusion, have appointed you to your inevitable tasks." Everywhere the intellectuals were strutting, posturing and declaiming, fancying themselves the new men of destiny. Few of them had an inkling that an industrial revolution, more fateful than the French Revolution, was brewing around them. Then one morning they woke up to discover that power had fallen into the hands of their middle-class relatives, their lowbrow brothers, uncles, in-laws, who not only had taken possession of everything they could lay their hands on, but wanted to impose their values and tastes on the whole of creation. The revulsion from a world dominated by the middle class alienated the intellectual from the machine age. Writers, poets, artists, philosophers and scholars poured scorn on the money-grubbing, mean-spirited, hard-working middle class, which aspired to master and tame God's creation. The doctrine spread that a genuine writer or artist must be at odds with his society; that alienation was a mark of intellectual nobility—an initiation into the mysteries of the universe.

Over a hundred years ago a Russian intellectual by the name of Pechorin wrote a poem on "how sweet it is to hate one's native land, and eagerly await its annihilation." Nikolai Berdyaev, who quotes Pechorin's poem in *The Russian Idea,* adds: "Only a Russian who loved his country passionately could write this." On the face of it this seems absurd, but when you remember the crucial characteristic of Russian history, Pechorin and Berdyaev begin to make sense. To a Russian who saw his country trapped in a succession of tyrannies, in a vicious circle which neither normal development nor revolutions could break, root and branch destruction was the only solution. A new foundation was needed. Alexander Herzen, a contemporary of Pechorin, was convinced that the industrialization and modernization of Russia would only reinforce the tyrannical system; that the achievements of science and technology would uphold "a Genghis Khan equipped with telegraphs, steamboats, ships and railroads." Progress was no cure, for the more Russia changed, the more did it remain the same. We see the same logical connection between love and hatred of one's homeland in Solzhenitsyn, Amalrik and others.

In a democratic country, hatred of one's native land cannot be fueled by a longing to escape a vicious circle of tyranny. Here the tearing down of the status quo clears the ground not for laying the foundation of a new freedom but for a dictatorship. We have seen it happen in Weimar Germany during the 1920s, when the adversary intellectuals' blind hatred played into Hitler's hands. One of these intellectuals, Kurt Tucholsky, had to run to Sweden when Hitler came to power, and it was in exile that he first realized the enormity of what he and his like had done to undermine Germany's first democratic society. He urged his fellow intellectuals to immerse themselves in a bath of self-criticism "in comparison with which sulphuric acid is like soap water." He eventually died by his own hand.

What is it then that drives some intellectuals in free

countries to hate their native land and wish for its anni-hilation? In a Western democracy the adversary intel-lectual is not only against his country and against the middle class into which he was born, but he sides with the colored races against the white, with animals against man, and with the wilderness against the sown. Predictably, an adversary intellectual who is a Jew sides with the Arabs against Israel.

Is this hatred of one's own a variant of self-hatred? Hardly so. One who hates what most people love proba-bly savors his uniqueness. He believes that secession from his country, class, race and species bespeaks right-eousness and partakes of the heroic. But above all he has an almost insane vanity. The adversary intellectual feels superior to the people who govern his country, but he will not run for office. He will not demean himself to beg the votes of stupid people. He lusts instead for an apocalyptic denouement that will topple the power structure and give him his chance.

The adversary intellectual cannot actually wreck a society, and he cannot seize power. But by discrediting and besmirching a society he undermines the faith of its potential defenders. When the Tucholskys had done their work, Weimar Germany could not defend itself against the wreckers—the communists and the Nazis.

In America up to a decade or so ago, the adversary stance of the alienated intellectual had not had a per-ceptible effect on national life. However, the post-sputnik education explosion, the civil rights and peace movements, and the anarchic consequences of affluence created both a potential following and a potential revolutionary situation, and the alienated intellectuals seemed finally to have come into their own. The literary-political salons of Manhattan and Washington are not unlike the salons of Necker's time, an "invisible power" which imposes its edicts on politicians, civil servants, judges, "concerned" business leaders, editors, publishers, teachers, students, reporters, broadcasters and literary and artistic coteries across the land.

Nowhere at present is there such a measureless loathing of their country by educated people as in America, and the savage denigration is undoubtedly undermining the faith of the country's potential defenders. But since there is no organized revolutionary force to do the wrecking, there has been no apocalyptic denouement. What we have instead is a society that has lost its nerve and is becoming feckless and confused. We have a society that cannot meet, let alone anticipate, challenges and has no goal to strive for and hardly anything worth fighting for.

The adversary intellectual savors power not by building or wrecking but by discomfiting and denigrating, and by rubbing the noses of the majority in dirt.

Change and Authority

In this country at present the people who clamor for drastic change are mostly hostile toward authority whether in government, family, school, factory or even in the armed forces. It seems to them logical that the flow of change would be less impeded in a permissive society. However, in human affairs the logic of events does not always correspond to the logic of the mind, and it is a fact that during the past hundred years drastic changes have been realized in more or less authoritarian atmospheres.

The changes experienced by Japan during the last third of the nineteenth century were more drastic and rapid than any the world had seen. In a few decades Japan went through an evolution for which the Occident needed centuries, yet in every department of life authority remained unquestioned or was even enhanced. The Japanese discarded overnight many of their most cherished values, illusions and skills without losing an atom of their confidence and self-righteousness. This seems incredible to us who have seen the failure of nerve of adults when drastic change disintegrated accepted values and made skills and experience obsolete.

Germany after 1870 is another instance of a country undergoing drastic change within an authoritarian framework. One has the feeling that in both Japan and Germany the men who engineered the programs of drastic change were aware of the need for vigorous authority.

In the Western democracies until recently, change in one field seemed compatible with stubborn conservatism in other fields. England managed to preserve social stability and continuity during the upheaval of the industrial revolution. In this country the vast economic changes after the Civil War were realized in an atmosphere of political and cultural conservatism. In France hectic political change went hand in hand with a stubborn resistance to change in the economy, the family and the school. Finally, the smoothest racial integration we have seen in this country took place in the army during the Truman administration when the old discipline was still in force.

It should be obvious that a society undergoing drastic change needs a strong framework of authority to hold it together, and an anchor of continuity to preserve its identity. Moreover, a drastic change is likely to be attended by unforeseen, explosive side effects which only a vigorous authority can prevent from vitiating and perverting the intended end result.

It has been a misfortune that the age-old Catholic Church chose to initiate unprecedented reforms at a time when so many countries were about to be racked and disoriented by drastic change. It was equally unfortunate that the Warren Court, which based its condemnation of school segregation on the findings of sociologists, had no social scientist to tell it how vital forceful authority would be to the achievement of racial integration. It is indeed remarkable how little thought social scientists have given to the role of authority in the realization of change. Two men who have touched briefly upon the problem come to mind. De Tocqueville, in *Democracy in America,* said that only a despot could solve America's racial problem, while Plato went to the extreme of maintaining that tyranny is the government under which change is easiest and most rapid.

Learning from Historians

It is surprising how little we can learn from historians at a time when history is exploding in our faces, so to speak. The cliché that he who would not learn from history is condemned to repeat it has been shown to be sheer bunk. It was the desire to learn from history that got us into one of the worst messes this country has ever been in. We got into Vietnam because we were determined to learn from history. We were convinced that had Britain and France done in Spain and Ethiopia during the 1930s what we were doing in Vietnam in the 1960s, there would have been no Second World War. We were in Vietnam to stop China and thus prevent a third world war. I cannot think of a single historian who told us in the early 1960s that the Russian-Chinese alliance was transitory and unnatural; that despite their common ideology the two were destined to become enemies. The historian, like the common run of the educated, stands in awe of ideology, of words, and ignores geography and human nature.

There were two old men, two nonhistorians, who strained their ears for the distant clang of a first clash between Russia and China. They were de Gaulle and Adenauer. Adenauer told visitors in the late 1950s to watch what the Russians were doing in Eastern Siberia —a territory of seven million square kilometers, not much smaller than China itself. De Gaulle was convinced that the Russians are "inherently racist. They are both racially and historically against the Chinese."

We know that the foremost historians can be incredibly wrong about the present. Sir Bernard Pares, Britain's leading expert on Russia, who for fifty years immersed himself in Russian history, and who had an intimate knowledge of the Russian people, was of the opinion that Stalin's regime was a nearer approach to true democracy than any of the liberal movements that preceded the revolution. He also believed that the purge trials were just.

We also know how wrong knowledgeable historians can be about the immediate future. Professor Pitirim Sorokin, who was born and raised in Russia, taught at both Russian and American universities, and wound up as chairman of the sociology department at Harvard University, predicted in 1944 that America and Russia, because of their "sociocultural similarities," would enjoy peaceful and even cordial relations after the end of the war. He expected America's cooperation with Russia to be closer than with any other country. Should either country commit one blunder after another, he reasoned, there might then be some temporary differences and quarrels, but these conflicts would remain minor. When postwar events proved him wrong, Sorokin insisted that his prognosis had been correct, but that the leaders of America and Russia had "committed the stupidest blunders in determining their mutual policies."

I can never forget something I heard on the San Francisco waterfront on V-J Day. There were wild celebrations on Market Street, but it was work as usual on the waterfront. I happened to work that day with two "Okies," two brothers from Oklahoma who were practically illiterate. As we were pulling the tarpaulins off the hatch, the older brother sounded off: "Now that we knocked out Japan, we will soon mix assholes with the Russians." It seemed to me the typical statement of an ignorant man. "What possible reasons," I asked, "could we ever have for fighting the Russians?" The Okie smiled tolerantly: "Have you ever watched boys playing on a sandlot? The moment one bully is down, you have to mix with the next one."

Events have proved the Okie right, and, for all I know, a sandlot may be the ideal model for the study of international relations. It may also be that the ignorant are better prophets than the learned. There is a saying in the Talmud that after the destruction of the temple prophecy was taken from the wise and given to children and fools.

Doing Good

There is the danger that one of the legacies of the turbulent 1960s will be a fear of doing good. The ills and
woes which beset our society at present, and strain it to
the breaking point, were born largely of an unprecedented effort to right wrongs and do good: to give
equality to the Negro, improve the lot of the poor and
throw open to all the gates of education and self-
improvement. The grotesque contrast between the
effort and the results is generating a mood not unlike
that which prevailed after the French Revolution: that
it is best to do no good so that one can do no harm.

The truth is that in human affairs there is no certainty
that good follows from good, and evil from evil. When
you start a course toward a desirable social goal, unpredictable side effects are likely to take over, and there is
no telling where the course will lead. It ought to be

clear, therefore, that when a society sets out to purge itself of iniquities it should expect the worst, and gird itself for a crisis that may test its stability and stamina. A just society must strive with all its might to right wrongs even if righting wrongs is a perilous undertaking. But if it is to survive, a just society must be strong and resolute enough to deal swiftly and forcefully with those who mistake its good will for weakness.

Michelangelo divided mankind into those who when you do them good get better, and those who get worse. Many beneficiaries of the civil rights and poverty programs obviously have belonged to the second category. The chronic have-nots who feel utterly worthless measure their power by the mischief they can cause. They see those who would do them good as either simpleminded or dishonest. It is of interest that most of the receivers of relief during the Roosevelt era belonged to Michelangelo's first category. They saw themselves as victims of the Depression, and felt that once things got back on the rails they would not only be able to help themselves but might eventually be in a position to help others. They were not chronic have-nots who see those who do them good as eternal creditors.

Finally, there is evidence that too many of the people who were carrying out the civil rights and poverty programs did not wish America well. Professor Aaron Wildavsky summarized the situation: "Middle-class civil servants hired upper-class student radicals to use lower-class Negroes as a battering-ram against the existing local political system." In other words, those in charge were less interested in healing and conciliating the weak than in aggravating their illness and sharpening their grievances. Thus, by a perverted dialectic, our wholehearted effort to right wrongs was shown to be proof not of our concern for righteousness but of our present and past incurable wrongness.

Black Studies

We are rarely reminded that the rush of European powers in the second half of the nineteenth century to grab colonies in Central Africa came at a time when armed bands of Arabs from Zanzibar were laying waste that part of the African continent in their search for ivory and slaves. Equipped with firearms, the Arabs looted ivory, grain and cattle, made slaves of the able-bodied natives, burned villages and wantonly killed those who did not escape into the bush.

Endless caravans of ivory-carrying slaves wound their way to the east coast. During the 1860s, seventy thousand slaves were sold annually in the Zanzibar slave market. It has been estimated that for every slave who reached the coast at least ten died of hunger, exhaustion and disease. The Arabs killed the slaves who lagged behind. One could trace the route of the slave caravan by the vultures and hyenas feeding on putrefying corpses. Had the Arabs been allowed to have their way for the balance of the century, much of Africa below the Sahara would have become an empty wasteland. It was the entrance of the colonial powers that brought to an end "the darkest days of Dark Africa."

The wanton cruelty of the Arab slave traders has been attested to by many explorers and travelers. David Livingstone, though befriended by a leading slave trader, Tippu Tib, was haunted in his last days by the horrors he had seen. In a late entry in his diary he tells of sights "so nauseous that I always strive to drive them from memory. But the slaving scenes come back unbidden and make me start up at dead of night horrified by their vividness." He called the Arab slave trade "this open sore of the world."

To an American there is poignancy in the fact that in the early 1860s, when the depredations of the Arabs were gathering momentum, hundreds of thousands of American soldiers died or were maimed to abolish Negro slavery in the United States. Yet many black Americans feel a greater affinity with the descendants of Arab slavers than with Americans whose forefathers fought one of the bloodiest civil wars in history to set the Negro free. How is one to explain this paradox? The answer generally given is that the Arab world has no Negro problem despite the fact that more black slaves were brought to Arab countries than to the North American

continent. The children of Arab masters and black con-
cubines were free. Black slaves became members of
their master's household and lived no worse than the
majority of Arabs. Such an answer, however, ignores
other, less benign, facts. Thus, most blacks in the Arab
world are members of the lower orders. And, according
to C. D. Darlington* the absence of a Negro problem in
the Arab world has genocidal undertones. "In general
it is clear that the Negro slave has been sterilized. Cas-
tration in meeting the demand for black eunuchs has
been one factor. Infanticide, abortion, perversion, both
homosexual and heterosexual, are other factors."

Yet it is doubtful whether these facts could affect the
pro-Arab leanings of American Negroes. For some ob-
scure reason they find it easier to identify themselves
with past masters than with those who champion their
cause. We are told that blacks feel more at home with
white people in the South than in other parts of the
country.

It is disconcerting that the unprecedented efforts to
right the Negro's wrongs have resulted not in an en-
hancement but in a diminution of America. The body
politic is less healthy after the operation of justice than
before. The tensions are higher, the grievances sharper,
the hopes dimmer.

*The Evolution of Man and Society, Simon & Schuster, 1971,
p. 350.

Nowhere in the world at present and at no time in the past has an underprivileged minority experienced such spectacular changes in its fortunes as did some twenty million Negroes in America during the 1960s. Yet we are not allowed to take pride in this unprecedented achievement. Negro spokesmen seem to believe that the Negro's cause will be advanced not by praising but by shaming America; that a proud, confident America would resist racial integration.

Organization

Several years ago I met a Yugoslav editor who visited
this country as a guest of the Department of State. He
was small, drab-looking, quite unlike the Yugoslavs I
have known on the waterfront. Mr. Tishma was pessi-
mistic about the future. Nationalism, he thought, was
getting stronger, and cooperation between nations
more difficult. Economic progress was slowed down by
the stubborn inertness of the masses. I told him that in
this country Yugoslavs form a competent and enterprising segment of the population. On the Pacific coast, in
particular, their organizing ability has been outstanding. Working with them through the years, I often won-
dered why such competent people should need a Tito
to tell them what to do. Mr. Tishma was aroused. "They
organize here," he shouted, "but they no organize
there." Which is probably true.

I asked myself what it was in this country that turned stubborn, inert Yugoslav immigrants into organizers. Was it the exceptional opportunities? Actually, they often created their own opportunities. They did pioneer work in grape growing and in fishing. Moreover, they displayed their organizing talent on the waterfront, where there was no question of exceptional opportunities. What was it, then? I brought up the subject when I met Jack Fischer, of *Harper's Magazine,* a man of great sagacity. He suggested that it might be a matter of trust. In the peasant society of Yugoslavia the air is heavy-laden with suspicion. You are on your guard all the time against ill will, meanness and trickery. You trust no one. The only form of united action possible in such a society is one imposed from above. On the other hand, in this country, from the very beginning, people have had to rely on each other in order to survive. Mutual trust and teamwork are integral to the style of life, and the talent for organization finds full scope.

It seems to me that Mr. Fischer's insight is particularly helpful when sizing up the strategies of the civil rights movement. There is no doubt that the Negro in America needs some sense of power in order to feel truly free and equal. How is he going to get it? Violence is not the answer because it is bound to result in either retaliation or apartheid. The Black Power agitation has done little more than bring notoriety to a few black loudmouths. No; the only way Negroes can savor power in this country is by organization. Organization, the accumulation of power without possession of the means of violence, requires not only patient, hard work, but trust among those to be organized. For a variety of reasons there is less mutual trust among Negroes than in the rest of the country; hence the creation of trust should be the first task of the civil rights leadership. This cannot be done by agitation and slogans. Negroes will begin to trust each other when they work together in successful cooperative enterprises. Negro cooperative efforts, inside and outside the city, are more vital to Negro progress than Negro private enterprise. The healing of the Negro's soul will come not from his integration with white people but from his integration with his fellow Negroes in thriving cooperative undertakings. And it may well be that, eventually, the confidence and self-esteem acquired by participation in a successful cooperative effort will make it possible for more Negroes to become effective capitalists.

Bernal Heights

I served for two years on the San Francisco Art Commission. His Honor Mayor Alioto assumed in his innocence that I might add luster to the commission. Actually, all I did at the monthly meetings was to say "Aye" when all in favor were supposed to say "Aye," and barely manage to keep my eyes open.

But I shall never forget one exciting meeting. There was a crowd of people in the back of the room when I arrived—a mixed group of whites and blacks, men and women, old and young, and of all hair lengths. We had had a crowd once before when a band of militants tried to intimidate the commission and snatch control of the purse strings. This time, however, there were no militants, and no designs on anyone's purse. The crowd came from Bernal Heights, a workingmen's neighborhood, where people of different ethnic backgrounds live side by side. There were whites, blacks, Chicanos, Samoans, Indians and some Chinese. The neighborhood has its share of loud-mouthed self-appointed spokesmen for minorities, but judging by what the crowd had to say, the militants are without a following. The people of Bernal Heights, most of them members of minorities, did not want to be minoritists. They wanted to be full-blown Americans, members of one nation indivisible, and to symbolize this common aspiration they had decided to paint their schoolhouse, situated on the top of a hill, red, white and blue. To do so they had to have the permission of the art commission, but our expert had vetoed the color scheme as garish. The crowd had come to put the case before the members of the commission and call for a vote.

They were well prepared. Their speakers spoke clearly and forcefully. The principal of the school spoke last. He was a middle-aged, gray-haired, neatly dressed, passionate Chicano, with a stars-and-stripes bow tie. He spoke of America the way a man speaks of the woman he loves. He had discovered America all by himself. It occurred to me as I listened to him that America is truly appreciated only by people who discover it. Some of us discovered America in the prison barracks of North Vietnam.

The commission voted unanimously to let the people of Bernal Heights paint their hilltop schoolhouse red, white and blue.

The Other Energy Crisis

It is worth noting that the Arabs, who are squatting on some of the world's largest pools of fossil fuel and can set off, at will, a crippling energy crisis in industrialized countries, have an energy crisis of their own which no amount of fuel can cure; namely, the meager flow of their human energies.

Through most of its history Islam has acted as a tranquilizer. It is a most congenial religion, without contradictions between state and church, profession and practice, the spirit and the flesh. The impressive mass calisthenics at prayer in spacious, carpeted mosques give the Moslem a profound sense of communion and egalitarianism. The result of this lack of contradictions and tensions has been intellectual and economic stagnation.

It is true that in its early phase, lasting about three

centuries, Islamic civilization was in the vanguard of mankind. But almost all the outstanding personalities of the Islamic renaissance were non-Arabs. They were Persians, Jews, Greeks, Berbers, Spaniards, and so notoriously impious that orthodox Moslems refused to break bread with them.

It is difficult to think of a religion more alien to the modern temper than Islam. It would be easier to modernize an animistic, primitive tribe than any Islamic country from Morocco to Indonesia. When in the early 1920s Kemal Atatürk, backed by nationalist enthusiasm, instituted drastic reforms which seemed to modernize Turkey overnight, it looked as though mass movements would be effective instruments for the renovation of Islamic countries. But in the 1970s it is obvious that despite the unprecedented reforms, Turkey is still backward and stagnant. Nor could Nasserism shake Egypt out of chronic stagnation despite the fact that Egypt has been in intimate contact with the Occident since the days of Mehemet Ali. It is also legitimate to doubt whether the massive importation of modern hardware will ensure the durable modernization of Iran. One wonders whether Islam's implacable hostility toward Israel may not stem partly from Israel's glaring demonstration that modernization is not achieved automatically by the acquisition of machines but requires ceaseless, hard work.

Should the decay of the work ethic and a shortage of

raw materials edge the Occident toward stagnation, it is still unlikely that the Islamic oil countries would be stirred to vault the narrowed gap into the twentieth century. The indications are that they will use their accumulated billions to bolster and spread the sway of Islam; to redress the balance between the Christian West and the Islamic East. There will be pressure against non-Islamic enclaves such as the Maronites in Lebanon, the Jews in Palestine, and the Chinese and Indian minorities in Southeast Asia. But the main effort will be directed toward the Islamization of Africa. Arab states are backing the Eritrean separatists in Ethiopia, and Moslems have seized power in Uganda, Chad and Nigeria. By an ironic twist of history, the nations of the Occident, which a hundred years ago ousted the Arab slave traders from the heart of Africa, are now being bled to finance a resurgence of Arab influence.

China

China was to the Far East what Greece and Rome combined were to the West. Like Greece in the West, China was the source of cultural life in its Far Eastern sphere —in Korea, Japan, Vietnam and Mongolia—and like Rome it served as a model for civil and military administration. Thus the rebirth of China cannot be viewed merely as an instance of something that is going on at present in the underdeveloped parts of the world. It is more as though Greece and Rome had come back to life, ready to dominate again the Mediterranean basin and Europe beyond the Alps.

Despite the striking differences between them, the Occident and China have fundamental qualities in common which set them apart from the rest of the world. We have tended to see the Occident's dynamism as unparalleled and unprecedented. The frenzied activity released by the industrial revolution seemed like a lone volcano erupting in a vast dead landscape. Yet during the past hundred years Chinese immigrants in Southeast Asia and the Japanese in Japan have demonstrated that the Chinese Far East has an inborn stamina, a capacity for self-starting, ceaseless effort comparable to that of the Occident. Indeed, at this moment the social vigor of the Chinese Far East seems more durable, and more likely to play a leading global role. An Englishman who leaves his crisis-ridden island and goes to Singapore is awed and shamed by the sight of Chinese enterprise and achievement, the disciplined Chinese vitality, amidst monuments of Britain's past greatness.

China's social vigor has deep roots in the past; in the ancient, well-organized and religiously conceived family system. The total identification with the family made the Chinese individual a tireless producer and reproducer in order to feed his family and ensure its immortality. Moreover, in a densely populated country where over 80 percent of the population made a living by intensive cultivation, which requires a tremendous amount of backbreaking labor, only families whose members were addicted to work could survive. Thus the work habit became innate, almost instinctive. From early days travelers have spoken of the Chinese as "working bees."

Reading Chinese history, one has the impression of an

inexhaustible human vitality. Already in the third century B.C. China formed the largest aggregate of human beings, as it does today. The Chinese weathered disasters that elsewhere destroyed societies. To an observer in the fourth century A.D., "it might have appeared that Rome would always endure but that the days of the Chinese Empire were definitely over." Yet by the middle of the fifth century barbarians were destroying Rome, whereas in China the barbarian invasion eventually resulted in a restored empire, stronger and richer than ever before.* In its long history China has experienced several declines and falls followed by rebirths to new greatness.

Linked with inborn stamina is the ability to borrow from other civilizations without ill effects. It is as though borrowing were a form of digestion, with only vigorous social bodies being able to digest and assimilate foreign matter. Actually, the ability to assimilate is a function of confidence. Societies lacking confidence see in imitation an act of submission and a proof of their inadequacy and inferiority. When the world was young, Egypt, India, Crete and others borrowed freely from Sumer, yet developed unique, vigorous civilizations. The Occident from its early days thrived on its borrowing from other civilizations, and China not only borrowed pro-

*E. O. Reischauer and J. K. Fairbank, *East Asia: The Great Tradition,* Houghton Mifflin, 1960, p. 148.

fusely but excelled in assimilating foreign races. Everywhere we look at present we see backward countries sickening on their borrowings from the Occident. So far, Japan is the only non-Occidental country that has managed to modernize itself in a hurry and is now able to vie with the model it imitated. The indications are that China, Korea, Vietnam and Mongolia will be able to recapitulate Japan's experience.

The contrast between Russia's and China's capacity to borrow is of absorbing interest. Russia is still suffering from the social indigestion it contracted when Peter the Great set in motion a massive imitation of the West. Later, the swallowing of the Western Marxist heresy aggravated the illness. On the other hand, China's prodigious ability to assimilate foreign elements ensures the success of any practice, doctrine or institution it borrows. It seems to be generally agreed that communism is more efficient in China than in Russia, and China is the only communist country that is producing enough to feed its people. If communism does not succeed in China it won't succeed anywhere.

The acclimatization of communism will not be impeded by the fact that it undermines the Chinese family system. A family-oriented society has a remarkable faculty for transplanting family relationships to other institutions—to factory, neighborhood, commune, army—and the weakening of blood ties is likely to intensify this faculty. Thus the Chinese Far East is becoming an ideal milieu for the development of esprit de corps—the creation of family ties between strangers —which in the world's present mental climate is the most durable source of social discipline and cohesion.

A Country
That Cannot Change

At a time when nations are changing their character almost overnight, there is one big country that has changed very little, if at all. Almost everything that was written, say thirty years ago, about Americans, Englishmen, Frenchmen, Germans, Japanese, Chinese, etc., is largely out of date. But de Custine's description of the Russians in 1846 is not appreciably different from Van der Post's description of them in 1963. This despite revolution, wars, fearful slaughter and momentous achievements.

In no other industrial country does the old live on in the new as it does in Russia. There is more continuity between Communist and Czarist Russia, and even Russia under the Tartar Khans, than between America in the 1970s and its past of a few decades ago.

Early in this century Sir Charles Dilke predicted that

no one alive would live to see a change in the system of Russian government. When it was objected that a revolution was surely possible, he answered: "Not only possible but very probable. There may be more than one revolution, but none of them will change the system of Russian government but will only replace one despotism by another." Indeed, the Russians have passed from tyranny to tyranny with no interval of freedom in between long enough to give them a taste of the exhilaration and the pains of an autonomous life. They have never been left to their own devices long enough to show what they could do on their own with no master to shove them around.

Can slaves evolve and change? Can there be turning points in their history such as the Renaissance, the Reformation, the Enlightenment, and the industrial revolution in the Occident, and the Meiji revolution and the Second World War in Japan? Whenever Russian history reached what seemed a turning point, it turned back.

Yet slaves can fight wars and conquer continents. They can create and invent. They can sing as free men never can. They can have deeper insights into men's souls, and greater power in depicting human destinies. No free man has ever praised freedom as eloquently as a noble-souled slave—for over a century the free Occident has been made aware of its most precious possessions by voices reaching it from the depths of Russia.

Slaves can have a richer, more luxuriating and more sheltered inner life than free men. Slaves can dream and hope, but they cannot change.

Can slaves tell the truth? "A Russian," said Leontiev, "can be a saint but not an honest man." All through the centuries lying has been a Russian specialty—lying not for gain but out of a dark fear of truth. In Soviet Russia lying has become a chief industry, wholly automated. To the Soviet leaders truth and treason are synonymous. Ambassador William C. Bullitt thought that when dealing with Russians, "no weapon is at once so disarming and effective as sheer honesty. They know very little about it." In Russia only great poets tell the truth, and in Russia poets are persecuted and killed.

The eloquent Africanist Laurens Van der Post, in his travels through Russia in the early 1960s, was struck by the similarity between the patient, submissive humanity he saw in Russia and the primitive black crowds he had seen in African railroad stations and public offices. He saw "the same silent acceptance of their fate implicit in the expression and attitude of these waiting figures." He began to suspect that one could not have a real understanding of Russian behavior unless one saw it as the expression of "an archaic, religious and profoundly superstitious system."

What then of the future? Would it be reasonable to look forward to a liberation of the Russian people at a time when freedom seems everywhere in retreat?

From its earliest attempts at modernization Russia both embraced and rejected the individualist West it was imitating. An overwhelming sense of inferiority breeds resentment against the superior model; and the more thriving the model seems, the more bitter is the resentment. We can apparently be at ease only when we imitate a defeated or dead model. Thus the decline of the West could figure as the most fateful event in Russian history.

Should the present double-barreled energy crisis (a shortage of fuel plus a revulsion from work) drain the Occident of its dynamism and mire it in a chronic depression, Russia may venture to experiment with democratic socialism and individual initiative as counterweights to a stifling bureaucracy. The first signs of such a venture would be likely to appear in Eastern Siberia, where the identification with the Occident is already fairly marked. Eventually Russia might cast itself in the role of a modern Occidental power wrestling with a primeval Chinese dragon.

The Tragic Sense

There was a time when I doubted whether tragedy was at all possible in America, and whether a person born and bred in this country could produce a genuinely tragic novel, play or film. Our equality is such that a comedown in the world cannot have the tragic import it has in other countries. In no other society are there so many topics on which people from every walk of life can talk with equal expertise. Moreover, the language of skid row or prison is not substantially different from the language one hears in a bankers' club or even in the White House. Thus a banker who lands on skid row or in prison finds life familiar enough not to feel wholly cast out. No matter how low one has fallen one can still argue, beef and laugh in the old manner.

However, the fact that a personal comedown cannot be as tragic here as in other countries became irrelevant when tragedy did come to America in the 1960s. In that terrible decade, the sober report of a day's events became the chronicle of individual and communal tragedies: the wasting of young lives by rebellion, drugs and drift; the despair of parents; the humbling of the deans and presidents of universities; the savage beatings of old men and women by murderous punks; the wreckage of two presidencies; the agony of a drawn-out, no-win war.

Though the war is now over, the campuses quiet and the presidency back on the rails, the tragic sense is still with us. We cannot defend our old against juvenile savagery in the big cities and we cannot safeguard our young. The erosion of traditional authority goes on and it is difficult to see how it can be stopped, let alone reversed. This is particularly true of the family. We are at the mercy of our children. They hold the threat of self-destruction over our heads and we are afraid to discipline them. The fallout of the 1960s is still contaminating family life in the 1970s. For although the counterculture has lost its epidemic thrust, it is still present and visible as an escape from the discipline of family, school and job. It is doubtful whether a society can be buoyant and hopeful as long as there are pitfalls and snares to decimate the young, and parents can do little to protect and direct their children.

Thus it looks as though the tragic sense will become a permanent part of our inner landscape. It will darken our spirit, but it may also deepen and mature our view of life. It may make us

> Face the world as a wise man should,
> And train for ill and not for good.

It may also expand our capacity for compassion.

Compassion

A most startling and fateful fact of our age is the non-fulfillment of the prophecy that a triumphant technology would make man superfluous. Though there is still talk about computers doing all the work and all the thinking, it is evident that impersonal factors do not shape and direct affairs in post-industrial society. Instead, we have entered a psychological age. As never before man is making history, and the enormities of Lenin, Stalin and Hitler have proved that man is the origin of all evil.

In the alchemy of man's soul almost all noble attributes—courage, honor, love, hope, faith, duty, loyalty—can be transmuted into ruthlessness. Compassion alone stands apart from the continuous traffic between good and evil within us. Compassion is the antitoxin of the soul: Where there is compassion even the most poisonous impulses remain relatively harmless. Thus the survival of the species may well depend on the ability to foster a boundless capacity for compassion.

Compassion seems to have its roots in the family. We think of those we love as easily bruised, and our love is shot through with imaginings of the hurts lying in wait for them. A loving wife cannot help imagining the wounds which a day's participation in the rat race may inflict on her husband, and he in turn senses the fears, born of unavoidable physical decline, which prey on his wife's mind. Their impulse is to protect, console and reassure each other. Parents overflow with compassion as they see their children go out into a strange, cold world.

It is conceivable that the present weakening of the family may allow compassion to leak into wider circles. So, too, the creation of family ties between strangers— esprit de corps—should aid the spread of compassion. But the question is whether we can make people compassionate by education.

It amazes me that well-educated people are not more compassionate than the uneducated. The reverse seems to be true. When Gandhi was asked what worried him most he replied: "The hardness of heart of the educated." The enormities of the twentieth century were committed by people who were better educated than the average and who felt competent to instruct and guide the ignorant. It was not far-fetched of Churchill to speak of the members of the Soviet politburo as "the bloody-minded professors of the Kremlin." There was a high percentage of schoolteachers among the Nazi Gauleiters. Among the twenty members of the group in charge of the extermination of the Jews there were a university professor, eight lawyers, a dental surgeon, an architect, an art expert and an ex-pastor.

It could well be that the adoption of a certain view of life would be fruitful of benevolence and compassion. We feel close to each other when we see ourselves as strangers and outsiders on this planet or see the planet as an island of life in a dark immensity of nothingness. We also draw together when we are aware that night must close in on all living things; that we are condemned to death at birth, and that life is a bus ride to the place of execution. All our squabbling and vying are about seats in the bus, and the ride is over before we know it.

Shame

The ancient Hebrews were alone in envisioning a troubled paradise. The Garden of Eden was not an abode of bliss but a place tense with suspicion and anxiety. For no sooner did God, in a moment of divine recklessness, create man in His own image than He was filled with misgivings. There was no telling what a creature thus made would do next. So God placed Adam and Eve in the Garden of Eden, where he could watch them.

It is plain that Adam and Eve were ill at ease under constant observation, and in their isolation from other living things. They welcomed the snake's visit, confided in him and listened to his advice. The expulsion from Eden was not the terrible fall it has been made out to be. It was actually a liberation from the stifling confines of a celestial zoo.

Now, what concerns me is the puzzling fact that

when Adam and Eve followed the snake's advice, diso-
beyed God's commandment and ate from "the tree of
the knowledge of good and evil," they felt not guilty but
ashamed—ashamed of their nakedness. What connection could there be between the knowledge of good and
evil and the impulse to cover the genitals with fig
leaves?

It is conceivable that, to begin with, good and evil
were not individual but social concepts. That was good
which preserved the group, and that evil which threatened its survival. Now, there is one dangerous threat
that no society can escape: namely, the recurrent threat
of disruption by juveniles as a young generation passes
from boyhood to manhood. Since sexual drives are at
the core of the destructive impulses characteristic of
the juvenile phase, sex is seen as a threat, hence an evil.
The primeval association of sex with shame is like the
taboos of incest and endogamy, part of an apparatus
devised to defend a society against rape by the juveniles
of the tribe. Through the millennia societies have acted
as if their safety depended upon the preservation of
female chastity.

Sex, of course, is not the sole threat to the group.
Cowardice, weakness, bad manners are as dangerous,
and they, too, are associated with shame.

Shame, far more than guilt, involves an awareness by
the individual of being watched and judged by the
group. It is to be expected, therefore, that the more

compact the group, the more pronounced the sense of shame. The member of a compact group carries the group within him and never feels alone.

Some anthropologists distinguish between the "shame culture" of primitive groups and the "guilt culture" of advanced societies. Actually, what comes here in question is not social primitiveness but social compactness. It is true that the most perfect examples of social compactness are found in primitive societies. But a technically advanced country like Japan, in which the individual is totally integrated with the group, has as strong a sense of shame as any primitive tribe.

By the same token one would expect the sense of shame to be blurred where socialization of the young becomes ineffectual, and social cohesion is weakened. In this country at present the inability of adults to socialize their young has made it possible for juveniles to follow their bents, act on their impulses and materialize their fantasies. The result has been a youth culture flauntingly, shameless. You see well-fed, good-looking youngsters, obviously the sons and daughters of well-to-do parents, begging in the streets, petting in public, lining up for pornographic movies and vying with each other to take advantage of every opening for skulduggery offered by a social system based on trust.

Even more disconcerting is the fact that the loss of shame is not confined to juveniles. The adult majority is not ashamed of its cowardice, workers are not ashamed of negligence, manufacturers of marketing shoddy products, or the rich of dodging taxes. We have become a shameless society.

Our intellectual mentors strive to infect us with a sense of guilt—about Vietnam, the Negro, the poor, pollution—and frown on shame as reactionary and repressive. But whether or not a sense of guilt will make us a better people, the loss of shame threatens our survival as a civilized society. For most of the acts we are ashamed of are not punishable by law, and civilized living depends upon the observance of unenforceable rules.

One also has the feeling that shame is more uniquely human than guilt. There is more fear in guilt than in shame, and animals know fear. We blanch with guilt as we do with fear, but we blush with shame.

The fabulous Greeks made of shame a goddess— Aidos. She was the source of dignity, decency and good manners. An offense committed against Aidos was avenged by the goddess Nemesis. Long live shame!

The Primacy of Man

There is probably in all professions some discrepancy between words and performance. Usually, the words are the more impressive and noble. But in the case of certain architects the opposite seems to be true: Their performance is more original and pregnant with meaning than their words. I know several excellent architects who usually speak feelingly and reverentially about nature; how we must harmonize and blend with nature and never violate it. To hear them talk you would think that if they built a house on the side of a hill they would so blend it with nature that you could not see the house until you bumped against it. Actually, they do no such thing. As genuine creators they know that harmony with nature must be achieved on human terms; that when they bring man and nature together man is the host and nature his guest. The primacy of man must be patent. When a gifted architect finishes his task, a gate built between two ancient trees will look as if the gate were there first and the trees planted afterward. If he builds a house over a creek, the beholder ought not to have the least doubt that the house was there first and the creek brought in later. You do not violate or demean nature by making her your guest. From the beginning of time trees, grass, flowers, birds and animals have felt wholly at home in human habitations, even the city, whereas nature has always been a stern and grudging host.

Whenever I talk with architects, I tell them about the British general Charles Granville Bruce, who when he first gazed at the prodigious massif of that great Himalayan peak Nanga Parbat, clad in eternal snow, felt that he wasn't there, and that it did not matter whether he existed. That a human being, the greatest prodigy of the universe, who has all continents, all oceans and all mountains within him, should feel that he doesn't exist when he gazes at a pile of mindless, soulless rock and snow seems to me outrageous. Architects, if they are any good, ought to be able to build a bungalow on the Himalayas so that Nanga Parbat and all the other peaks would seem but a background for it. Pascal expressed it beautifully: "All the bodies, the firmament, the stars, the earth are not equal in value to the lowest human being. From all bodies together not the slightest thought and not a single impulse of charity can be obtained."

I also find my own experience reflected in the saying of another Frenchman, Henry de Montherlant: "However wonderful the stars may be, I still prefer the light made by man." Compare this with the words of the great humanitarian Bertrand Russell: "The sea, the stars, the wind in waste places mean more to me than even the human beings I love best." I can guess, more or less, what Russell felt when he listened to the wind in waste places. He was lifted out of the paltriness and transitoriness of an individual existence by communion with nature's eternal recurrence, and by feeling one with sea, stars and the whispering wind. But it may fare ill with mankind if ever power falls into the hands of the Bertrand Russells.

A society's attitude toward nature affects its whole pattern of life. In India nature is as savage as it is on this continent, but the attitude toward nature is the opposite of ours. Indian humanity feels itself the plaything and the slave of the fearful forces which it worships and tries to propitiate. Freedom and deliverance can be gained only by ceasing to be human. Indian religion and philosophy side with nature against man. A worm must not be killed, but in Calcutta children are sprawled dead on the pavement and no one pays attention. Man is the cheapest commodity on the Indian subcontinent. It is a truth we find difficult to accept that India is not a place where man feels compassion for his fellow men.

To us nature is not the image of God but His handiwork. Jehovah created the world, but He made man in

His own image. Our cocky attitude toward nature has its roots in the downgrading of nature by the ancient Hebrews. Freedom to us means, basically, freedom from the iron necessities and implacable determinism which dominate nature. We are hostile toward absolute power because it gives to commands the inexorableness of laws of nature. We believe that a society awed by nature cannot be free because it equates power with nature and would no more revolt against despotic power than it would against a natural calamity.

Unavoidably, one wonders whether the receptivity of present-day young to Hindu cults betokens a changed attitude toward nature. Many of the young, particularly the children of well-off and well-educated parents, have been made aware of the possibility of a nuclear holocaust from the day they were born. They see the poisonous mushroom cloud as nature's retaliation against the violators who stole her secrets. The ecological fervor is probably the manifestation of an urge to propitiate nature. And although the ecological concern is all to the good, the young's attitude toward nature should fill us with foreboding. On this savage continent, anyone who sides with nature against man—as many of the wilderness boys do—ought to have his head examined.

Rebirth

It is conceivable that new and finer values are being created and cultivated by the young who have come through the ordeal of juvenility more or less whole. There is this beautiful camaraderie among the young and a readiness to share with one another. The young are mostly free of snobbishness and racial prejudice. There is also a new concern with the environment and with quality of life. Nevertheless, the majority of us are overwhelmed by the loss of much that has made this country great, and our fear is more potent than our hope.

Consider what has happened to us: An America that fought two wars simultaneously and was victorious both in the Pacific and in Europe; that gave billions to rebuild Europe and Japan; that pushed through the second industrial revolution and gave its people a taste of

unimagined plenty; that plunged into an unprecedented attempt to right all wrongs overnight—an
America that has done all these things and also landed
the first man on the moon wakes up one morning and
finds itself weirdly diminished. It finds its dollar de-
valued, its natural resources seriously depleted, its ethnic minorities climbing out of the melting pot, its youth
alienated, its armed forces demoralized, its manufac-
tures shoddy, its workers negligent, its history be-
smirched by revisionist historians, its cities decayed and
stewing in crime, its air and water polluted, and its
leaders drained of confidence. Is it any wonder then
that many of us are bewildered, a prey to doubts and
fears about the future?

The nagging question is whether we can recover the
virtues we have lost. Is social decline reversible?

It is easier to turn free men into slaves than slaves into
free men; easier to lose the readiness to work than to
acquire it; easier to lose courage than to regain it.
Deterioration is a downhill slide, while reversion seems
an uphill climb. There are some who question the possibility of reversing social decline. "No social policy," says
de Tocqueville, "has yet been devised to make an energetic people of a community of pusillanimous and en-
feebled citizens." Dean Acheson could not recall "an
instance of a democratic society that once having lost
the will to provide for domestic tranquillity and national security has regained it by a new birth of discipline and commitment."

Actually, the past hundred years have seen many instances of the transformation and rebirth of societies. Germany and Japan renovated themselves in the last third of the nineteenth century and brought about a spectacular rise in the morale of millions. It is true that these changes were realized in an authoritarian atmosphere. However, equally remarkable changes in morale took place in democratic France at the turn of the century. Around 1890, France seemed played out: low birth rate, military weakness, alcoholism, morbid eroticism, decadent trends in literature and in the arts, and a plague of anarchist bombings which culminated in the assassination of President Sadi Carnot. Yet fifteen years later everything changed almost overnight. The young generation turned its back on decadence, made a cult of physical fitness, directed its energies toward science and technology, and became aggressively nationalist.

During the 1930s Hitler turned a demoralized Germany into an unequaled instrument of aggression, and later Mao Tse-tung, in less than two decades, transformed 800 million demoralized Chinese into a proud, disciplined nation. Clearly, the reversion of decline is not only possible but may proceed at breakneck speed.

Our own past also offers examples of the recovery of lost virtues. In 1976 we shall celebrate—not too heartily, I am afraid—the two hundredth anniversary of the founding of this country, and it may be reassuring to look back a hundred years to the state of the union in

1876. What do we find? We find a whole nation up to its nose in a morass of corruption. Not only the robber barons but people in every walk of life wallowed in crookedness. Crooks on a grand scale were folk heroes, and anecdotes about them pushed out of currency the earlier myths of Franklin, Washington and the founding fathers. Charles Francis Adams described the mood in his autobiography: "Failure seems to be regarded as the one unpardonable crime, success as the all-redeeming virtue, the acquisition of wealth as the single worthy aim of life. The hair-raising revelations of skulduggery and grand-scale thievery merely incite others to surpass by yet bolder outrages and more corrupt combinations." Nevertheless, the wholesale depravity did not have lasting effects. There was something that kept corruption from harming the social fiber. What was it? Hope. The air was tense with hope, with unbounded faith in the future. What one did in the present did not matter because the present was a mere mat on the doorstep of the future, something that would be thrown away and forgotten. Hope immunizes a society against degeneration and decay. Where there is no hope even the moral equivalent of sniffles may prove fatal.

What then could possibly be America's hope at present? The answer is not easy. The present is probably a watershed in the history of mankind. I cannot think of any time in the past when there were so few certainties, when so little could be taken for granted. Every value is being questioned, and most of the aspirations that animated humanity through the millennia have lost their lure. The promise of freedom, justice, peace, abundance and technological miracles can no longer stir minds and hearts.

I believe that a potent hope must be linked with the most critical challenge that is facing us. For the vigor of a society is demonstrated by how it responds to a challenge. Flabby societies refuse to see a challenge until it hits them in the face, while vigorous societies welcome a challenge as a spur to creative action. By this test the Western democracies, despite their hustle and glitter, are lacking in vigor. The quadrupling of the price of oil took them by surprise and they refuse to face the possibility that the age of fossil fuels is drawing to a close. They are dispirited, confused and frightened, ready to sell their soul for a barrel of oil. Nowhere in the Occident is there the will and the vision to make the energy crisis the opening act in a drama of renewal and rebirth.

Yet destiny seems to be on our side. It has been preparing us for the present trial and has been pointing the way to the right solution. To me it seems providential that a disenchantment with a high standard of living, particularly among the young, preceded the energy crisis. It was a fateful discovery of the 1960s that abundance does not bring peace of mind, does not release creative energies and does not maintain social stability. The oil shortage is giving meaning to the widespread inclination toward a simpler and more frugal life.

Even as we mobilize our scientific and technological know-how in a search for a cheaper and cleaner fuel, we ought to welcome the probability that the new fuel will not be in plentiful supply until the end of the century, and that the intervening twenty-five years of scarcity and unemployment can give us time to repair the damage done to our human and natural resources. We ought to see it as providential that millions of unemployed workers are now available to cleanse lakes and rivers of pollution, reforest the mountains, replenish the soil and renew the big cities by giving them spacious squares and parks. If we accept the challenge, the common effort and the common vision will unite us as never before, and America will again become a land of hope as a whole nation watches the gradual cleaning up of a continent and the progress made in the laboratories.

The danger is that we shall not get off the treadmill; that by threats and bribes we shall somehow manage to hang on to the fossil-fuel tit for decades and go on wanting what we no longer really want. It is this lingering, debilitating crisis that we have to fear most.